HIGHLY ACCLAIMED

"I have studied the book and I liked particularly the chapter 'The lightness of being' and the lines – Last but not the least is the big delusion... that the ego-self is the 'doer'."

– A. P. J. Abdul Kalam,
Former President, Republic of India

Stop Sleepwalking Through Life! is secular in its appeal and happily free from Hindu esoteric ideas (for the lay like me) like 'Upanishadic, Brahman' and associated Vedantic jargon. At the same time, there is unobtrusive assimilation of all the lofty thoughts found in our ancient teachings.

– A. S. Padmanabhan, IAS,
Former Chief Secy. To Govt. of Tamil Nadu

"I found this to be very educative... In particular, the idea that 'we should enjoy the present rather than worry about the future' ... Also, the conflicts of the ego-self are brought out clearly; these are the conflicts that we as teachers and coaches need to continually work to resolve in today's highly competitive world."

– M. Krishnakumar,
Management Consultant
and Tennis Coach, Kinesis, Bangalore

"This book takes the mystery out of the awakened mind and provides a context in which to utilize its teaching of awareness, in one's everyday life experiences."

– Patt Lind-Kyle,
Author of *When Sleeping Beauty Wakes Up*

Stop Sleepwalking Through Life! resembles the content that one would find in the Upanishads, Zen Buddhism, Taoism or the teachings of Ramana Maharshi and J. Krishnamurti.

The challenges faced by humankind in the 21st century require the inner awakening that Dr. Menon writes about. Reading the book would be an excellent start, to be followed by reflection, discussion and personal exploration/validation.

– Sudhir Krishna,
IIT Madras alumnus 1976

In this invaluable little book he questions the way we lead our lives. Having raised these questions, this book does not provide readymade prescriptive answers like many of the self-help books. This I think is the uniqueness of this book... I strongly recommend this book for anyone who is feeling restless in life and is sincerely seeking peace of mind, happiness and contentment.

– Dr. R. Gopinath, Bangalore,
http://bookwormsrecos.blogspot.com

"This book seeks to arouse the discerning intellect dormant among most human beings, and thus address a vital goal of education. It must, in my opinion, be the first book on any course in collegiate education. I have used the book in some of my courses and I have found that it has helped my students get out of the slumber, and identify a destiny and a destination."

– Prof. Shreesh Chaudhary,
Humanities & Social Sciences, IIT Madras, Chennai

"This book is a brilliant piece of work, especially commendable for the sheer lucidity with which the metaphysical dimension is presented. I enjoyed it immensely."

– Subir Chakraborty, Chief (Marketing),
SF Division, Exide Industries Ltd., Kolkata

"I haven't read anything more truthful and refreshing. I guess when truth strikes, it strikes hard."

– R. Shiv Shanker, University of Illinois,
Urbana-Champaign, USA

"This book helped me realize how much I was in the grip of my ego-self. I found it particularly relevant because of all the academic allusions. The last two chapters are absolutely exquisite."

– Prof. Bharath Sethuraman,
California State University, Northridge, USA

"This is a wonderful thought-provoking book which de-stresses the mind. It is a 'must-read' book for all in the teaching profession."

– Prof. B. S. Murty (Civil Engg.),
IIT Madras, Chennai

"Now and then a book comes along that makes you pause and compels you to take stock. This is one such book. Its insights seem true, not because of any underlying logic, but because deep down you already know them to be true. Succinctly put and hard-hitting."

– Siddharth Savadatti, Design Engineer,
Larsen & Toubro, Chennai

"It is a simple but incisive unfolding of how to stop shuttling between achieving dreams, punctuated by commas, and attain that one-stop dream which gives an infinite sense of fulfilment."

– Prof. Rekha Rau,
K. J. Somaiya Institute of
Management Studies and Research, Mumbai

"For those of us who have spent many years in teaching and counselling bright young people, this book comes as a blessing. In simple language, it shows how to gain an inner awareness which brings peace, uniting us to each other and to the whole universe. Its most valuable lesson is that a practical spirituality is possible within everyone's daily activities, including the pursuit of a successful career."

– Fr. Lancy Pereira S.J.,
Former Principal, St. Xavier's College,
Ex-Director, Caius Research Lab, Mumbai

"I encountered this book at the right moment in my life. It really made me stop and think. I go back to it again and again to find answers to many questions in life."

– R. Pandia Raj, M.S. Research Scholar,
IIT Madras, Chennai

"It was a totally engrossing read. At least during the reading time, I was able to see through the camouflage called 'ego-self' to discover and awaken its dormant counterpart, the 'pure-self', and experience some moments of quiet bliss."

– Praveen Mookoni, Software Consultant,
Fidelity Investments, Boston, USA

"I thoroughly enjoyed this wonderful book. The way Dr. Menon unfolds the mysteries of minds caught in the vortex of present-day materialism is lucid and enlightening. This book is a great treasure and I recommend it wholeheartedly to everyone for awakening and re-energizing."

– P. Y. Manjure, Director,
The Freyssinet Prestressed Concrete Co. Ltd., Mumbai

Stop sleepwalking through life !

9 LESSONS TO INCREASE
YOUR AWARENESS

DEVDAS MENON

YogiImpressions®

STOP SLEEPWALKING THROUGH LIFE!
First published in India in 2004 by
Yogi Impressions LLP
1711, Centre 1, World Trade Centre,
Cuffe Parade, Mumbai 400 005, India.
Website: www.yogiimpressions.com

First Edition, August 2004
Tenth reprint, February 2023

Cover illustration: Prabhakar Wairkar
Cover concept and interior book design: Shiv Sharma

ISBN 978-81-88479-51-1

Printed at: Manipal Technologies Limited

CONTENTS

FOREWORD

This is a 'spiritual' book with none of the jargon or technical terms that often scare away prospective readers from reading such books. This fact makes it special, and different from many other books on spirituality. Its main feature is that it is free from 'impressive incomprehensibility' and pedantry. Another special feature of this book is the highlighting of a higher dimension in education, which appears to be completely missing in the modern world, and which India was renowned for in ancient times.

Some people seem to believe that spiritual awakening is at variance with excellence in performance in the material world. The author of this book, Dr. Devdas Menon, by his personal example as a successful consultant and professor of structural engineering at IIT Madras, bears ample testimony to the fact that this is not so. All indications are that spirituality does improve the quality of whatever work is undertaken.

Dr. Menon is well-exposed to the various traditions of spirituality represented by Buddhism, Zen, Vedanta, Taoism, Christianity and Sufism, and has a special preference for the teachings of Ramana Maharshi,

Chuang Tzu, J. Krishnamurti, Nisargadatta Maharaj, and now Eckhart Tolle. He has received guidance from some highly evolved persons, a fact that will be evident upon reading this book. As the focus of this book is not on the author, and not even on the contents of the book, but decisively on the reader - spirituality is about the subject, and not the object - it is not proper to write much more. The less said, the better.

Dr. Menon's brilliant and popular lectures, which I have attended during the past two decades, have been peppered with some of the ideas expressed herein. This book is an outcome of persuasion by many of his friends, including myself, to articulate his insights in a logical order and publish them in a popular book form, so that many more people may be benefited.

I consider it a special privilege to have been called upon to write this Foreword, and I thank him sincerely for this honor.

Dr. K. B. M. Nambudiripad - Dean (Academic Affairs),
Amrita Vishwa Vidyapeetham, Ettimadai,
Coimbatore, India

25 December, 2003

ACKNOWLEDGMENTS

I did not plan to write this book. It just 'happened'.

I wish to acknowledge the tremendous support, inspiration and encouragement given by the following, in enabling this 'happening':

A. D. Pisharody, K. B. M. Nambudiripad, K. Krishnamurthy, Ahalya Chari, Bharath Sethuraman, S. Achyuthan Nair, V. Kalyanaraman, Radha Sarma, Gautam Sachdeva and Shiv Sharma.

I am grateful for the support given by my colleagues and students at IIT Madras, and other institutions in India and abroad.

Finally, I wish to express my love and gratitude to my parents, my teachers, and my dear wife, Roshni.

A young Apollo, golden-haired,
Stands dreaming on the brink of strife,
Magnificently unprepared,
For the long littleness of life.

Rupert Brooke

1

THE BIG DREAMS IN LIFE

"What is the *big dream* in your life?" I asked my class of undergraduate second year students at IIT Madras, a few years ago.

The 'young Apollos' gave me responses like: *"a genius the world will never forget"*, *"a world-famous academician"*, *"a billionaire in Silicon Valley"*, *"the CEO of a giant multinational company"*, etc. With the exception of a couple of responses, the ambitions of the majority were loud and clear. One student expressed it rather poetically: *"to have my name etched in gold in the shifting sands of time!"*

I went down memory lane, to some twenty-five years ago, and saw myself sitting in the same classroom at IIT Madras. The scene looked unbelievably the same. It seemed as though time stood still. The dreams seemed no different except, perhaps, that they were now being expressed more forcefully. These kids appeared less doubtful and more focused.

Like their seniors, most of them are headed for the United States, *the promised land*, and they know that nothing can stop them from achieving their ambitions. They believe that they are the brightest and the best in today's technology-driven world, and have good reason to do so. During the 2002 Golden Jubilee celebrations of the Indian Institutes of Technology (India's premier institutes of higher education), inaugurated by Bill Gates in California, the world came to know that "gaining admission to the IITs was more difficult than getting into the best Ivy League schools in the United States."

(*Source:* CBS News)

What happens when the big dreams get fulfilled? What happens when you become rich and famous? Will you attain an enduring state of fulfilment? Will you then be able to live happily ever after? Or, will there be something vital missing, something that you need to address now, when you are young and full of life? Is there not a deep truth in the saying of Jesus: *"For what does it profit a man, if he shall gain the whole world, and lose his own soul?"*

When I pose these basic questions to the students, they feel uncomfortable – but usually not sufficiently to seriously question their direction in life. The majority are too heavily programmed; one cannot really blame them for their strong sense of insecurity, discomfort, and inability to address the questions. There appears to be too much at stake in the rat race of life, and it takes considerable courage, even just to pause and reflect, especially when one has traveled far and got ahead in the race. It becomes even more difficult, if not impossible, as one grows older. The dreams of our brightest and best students are ones that have been consciously and unconsciously ingrained in them by social conditioning, by their parents and teachers. Their dreams are but a direct reflection of the prevailing materialistic world-view.

There is little in their education to persuade them to think otherwise. Everywhere, they see the extraordinary emphasis on competitive performance, on getting ahead of others. These kids have sweated it out to be way ahead of others. They, and the institutions that nurture them, are the leaders of the pack, the role models for the rest to emulate.

Is this the best our education has to offer today? Are we not completely evading certain key issues in life? Are we not leaving our young students "*magnificently unprepared, for the long littleness of life?*" as Rupert Brooke puts it so eloquently.

Most people are asleep; they live asleep,
Marry asleep, breed children in their sleep,
And die in their sleep, without ever waking up,
Never understanding the loveliness of existence.

Anthony de Mello

THE LONG LITTLENESS OF LIFE

The big dreams in life are actually few: getting through an entrance exam, securing a dream job, getting married, obtaining a 'green card', reaching the top of the ladder of success. These are but turning points in our life, which often signify the culmination of great struggles. Every accomplishment certainly brings us some sense of fulfilment but this, unfortunately, does not linger long. At no point can one stop, or even slow down, and feel: '*Yes, at last, I have found enduring happiness.*'

The little day-to-day things are the ones that dominate our lives. More often than not, we get so caught up in our daily chores that we barely remember our big dreams. Life moves at a hectic pace and, although we are somehow kept busy throughout the day, we may have little to show by way of accomplishment, and this is a source of daily dissatisfaction. We complain of too many distractions that prevent us from focusing our energies productively. The moments of creativity that we may experience at work are, for most of us, too few and far between.

Our interactions with people at the workplace and at home are not always pleasant. Frustrations, irritations, jealousies and clashes recur all too frequently, and these leave scars in our minds. We tend to become suspicious of people, and freely pass mental judgments on everyone in sight. Conversely, we also become vulnerable to other people's opinions and judgments, although we may pretend not to care. Our state of mind is often completely at the mercy of circumstances, at the way other people behave or fail to behave. Even an innocuous or stray remark can expose the fragility of our sense of well-being.

I was told the other day of one such incident involving a middle-aged lady. It happened to be the lady's birthday, and she was really happy to be woken up by her husband in the morning with birthday wishes and flowers. In a happy mood, she went out for her usual morning walk. But her happiness proved to be short-lived when she ran into a neighbor, who remarked: "Hi! You've been walking like this for months together, but instead of losing weight, you seem to be putting on weight!" The poor lady cut short her walk, locked herself up in her room, wept for two hours, and remained depressed the whole day.

We all have different reasons to feel depressed, and what may seem trivial to one person can be very serious to another. The mind has its own mechanics, and it does not obey the cold logic of reason. Small, unconnected but disconcerting events may cause our anger or depression to accumulate quietly, and suddenly, we may take it all out on someone vulnerable, our reaction being totally out of proportion with the apparent cause.

When we are so susceptible to such little tremors in our daily lives, how much more vulnerable will we become when some really big crisis hits us!

Life, of course, is not always that bad. We do have our moments of fun, don't we? Unfortunately, we cannot cling to them for long. It is probably more correct to state that, more often than not, we are neither happy nor sad. However, that intermediate state is frequently marked by listlessness, boredom or unease. I recall a very perceptive description of this mental state by a former student: "There is a deep sense of insecurity, a kind of nagging fear, that keeps popping up every now and then, although we do our very best to cover it up." One common way of covering it up is by continually engaging in some activity or other, even if it is routine and monotonous. We end up, consciously or unconsciously, doing all kinds of daily tasks, none of which may enthuse us. The drudgery of doing something mundane is often decidedly preferable to not doing anything at all. But even while engaging in physical activity, our minds are rarely focused on the job at hand. The mind is like a monkey, always distracted and disturbed.

Have we not been warned: 'an idle mind is a devil's workshop'? When there is nothing to do, and no company to gossip with, we tend to fidget. We crave for some distraction or the other. The TV remote and the cell phone prove to be handy instruments that relieve us somewhat from our boredom. We often need something really sensational, like an action-packed movie, to feel a sense of aliveness.

We human beings have the dubious distinction of undergoing untold suffering, including boredom, caused by our own minds. Look around you, and you can see everywhere that man, although endowed with more abilities than other living creatures, is ironically more discontent. Wise men in the past have suggested that this discontentment is nature's way of saying to the intelligent human being, "*something's wrong with you*" and, thereby, enabling one to awaken to a higher level of consciousness. But very rarely do we view life with this spirit of learning. It is very difficult for the 'normal' person to believe that the problem, if any, lies in him or her, and not in others or in the external circumstances.

When we have suffered enough, or when we are lucky to gain a sudden insight, we may awaken to the truth and discover a deeper dimension to life – one that promises an incredible freedom from the 'long littleness of life'.

Then, awakened, one can experience the *loveliness of existence* that Anthony de Mello refers to. One then becomes the ideal teacher and the ideal parent. But, first, one has to awaken. It is an awakening from a deep-rooted spiritual ignorance regarding one's very identity. A quiet joy then replaces the underlying unease.

There is a nice story on awakening or the lack of it, a story about the chicken and the eagle, made popular by Anthony de Mello. Once upon a time, there was an eagle's egg that somehow got lost and got mixed up with the eggs of a hen. The eggs hatched, and the eaglet grew up with a brood of chicks. The eaglet believed it was a chicken (although it did look rather awkward to other chickens), and it lived all its life doing what the other chickens did. It clucked and cackled, and scratched the earth for insects and worms. It could even fly up a few feet into the air, thrashing its wings about like the other chickens.

Many years later, on a bright cloudless day, the eagle-chicken saw a magnificent bird high above in the sky. With its wide wings fully spread out, the great bird glided effortlessly and majestically. Awed by this sight, the eagle-chicken asked "Who's that?" and a wise old hen replied, "*That's the eagle, the king of the birds. The great eagles live in the sky; but we chickens can live only on the earth.*" And so, the eagle that believed it was a chicken, lived like one and eventually died like one, without ever realizing its true identity and potential.

Awakening does not figure in the list of big dreams in life for most of us – not yet, anyway. Many of those dreams are identifiable with whatever it is that causes envy in others, and awakening implies, among other things, an immediate freedom from this stupid obsession. Also, awakening is not something to be pursued in the distant future in some remote place. It is something to be realized here and now, in almost everything that we do.

If we do not choose to awaken, we will continue to sleepwalk through life.

The birth of a man is the birth of his sorrow,
The longer he lives, the more stupid he becomes,
His thirst for survival and happiness in the future,
Prevents him from living in the present.

Chuang Tzu

3

EVASION OF FIRST PRINCIPLES

Not many people may approve of the verse on human stupidity conceived by the great Chinese sage, Chuang Tzu, some twenty-five centuries ago. The lines sound too depressing, don't they? But they contain many truths, and if these truths appear bitter, they do so because we have been evading them for centuries. Some of us may even be inclined to deny any truth in these lines that appear to be so pessimistic. However, truth has nothing to do with pessimism or optimism; truth is just simple truth.

I once asked the students in my class: "Supposing you fell ill, and the doctors detected that you had a serious cancer. Would you like to be informed of it or not?" The majority of the students chose to respond with a loud "*No!*" Only a few were brave enough to say "*Yes!*" Some of the cleverer ones said: "*Yes, but only if the cancer is curable.*"

We may excuse these students for not being willing to accept the bitter truth; they may not yet have fully 'grown up' and matured. But, perhaps, age has nothing to do with this, because the vast majority of fully-grown adults are not any different. Any mention of death, for instance, is considered in our society to be 'morbid' or inauspicious, even though it is a perfectly natural and unavoidable fact of life. The older we grow, the more we seek to evade this one certain truth in life, and the more we seek to ensure our permanence by clinging to our possessions and pursuing happiness in the future, not knowing what it means to live in the present. This is certainly not a sign of intelligence, and if Chuang Tzu squarely refers to it as *stupidity*, how can we find fault with him? If we were not stupid, we would seek to understand the meaning of death and impermanence and, thereby, perhaps discover a deeper meaning to life.

If we are 'magnificently unprepared', it is apparently by choice.

But, is not the human species gifted with great intelligence? Surely, the great achievements of science and technology in the last three centuries bear ample evidence to this. Take, for example, the great advances in medicine and the promise of genetic engineering, that enable man to play God. Increasing longevity, preserving beauty in the body, slowing down ageing – are these not wonderful things that men and women crave for, now possible thanks to man's genius? Hardly anyone asks: "*Of what use is prolonging life in the body? What indeed is the purpose of human life? What is death and why do we fear it so much?*"

If prolonged survival is considered a measure of intelligence of a species, we had better come to grips with a really bitter truth. Perhaps even Chuang Tzu may not have visualized, twenty-five centuries ago, the progress in the human ability to annihilate, from a few hundreds to entire civilizations. His comment aimed at individual human stupidity is being vindicated by the entire human species. Indeed, there is increasingly less evidence to show that human intelligence and sanity can be trusted to avoid the usage of weapons of mass destruction. The survival of all life forms on earth is now under threat, as never before.

As a human species, we remain 'magnificently unprepared' for this eventuality.

We invariably evade or postpone our reflections on the deeper issues in life, because we believe that we are too busy with things that are of immediate consequence. This is true even in the academic world of intellectuals and scientists. We may hold doctorates in philosophy (Ph.Ds), and be keen on questioning and pursuing the fundamental principles in our various narrow fields of specialization, but we evade the fundamental questions that pertain to our very basic nature. We accept the ways and illusions of the world.

The scientist or academician may choose to believe that he is intellectually superior to the common businessman, but in today's world, academicians are just different kinds of businessmen. Just as the businessman identifies his sense of self almost completely by the value of his total material assets, the academician's identity and worth are defined in terms of his designation, publications, research funding, patents (intellectual property rights), awards, and memberships to elite societies. Gone are the days when knowledge was pursued for the sake of knowledge, purely for one's own edification, and simply to satisfy an inherent quest for truth. Most researchers today have to reconcile with the fact that, in order to get ahead in life, they may need to do work in areas that are uninteresting and sometimes unethical, just because money is available, or because it is relatively easy to publish or patent. The 'rat race' culture has spread its tentacles everywhere, including the portals of the academic world, where the *mantra* today is: '*Publish or perish*'. Nobody seems to care for the higher truth: '*Awaken or perish*'.

The erudite scholar is as vulnerable as anybody else, if not more, to common human failings such as greed, envy, manipulation, pretension, anger, and fear. Erudition has done little to bring liberation from these failings.

The suffering and humiliation that a brilliant scientist or intellectual or artist undergoes when, year after year, he finds himself overlooked for a prestigious award, can be very severe. Furthermore, it is like adding insult to injury when a less deserving colleague wins the award; the pain can become unbearable.

How ironical it is that extreme brilliance can coexist with extreme stupidity in the same individual! How ironical it is that with growing age, education, and experience, one may gain tremendous knowledge and yet remain actually unwise!

Nevertheless, even in the academic world, a few do entertain the belief that some day, perhaps after retirement, they can sit down and ponder on the deeper issues in life, and maybe get awakened. Until then, it is very much: '*business as usual*'.

Why is it that we evade questioning the fundamental perceptions that form the very basis of our existence, our paradigm for living? Is it because of some deep-seated fear that, should we ponder on these issues, we may possibly end up as useless philosophers or in the lunatic asylum? The time and energy spent on this could retard our progress in life, and we might fall behind in the rat race. Apparently, we have no choice but to accept the ways of the world. Besides, so many people cannot possibly all be wrong.

But even when we are on the verge of so-called 'retirement' (which we dread), we remain 'magnificently unprepared'. We look out for alternative means of gainful employment, thereby postponing the inevitable. When the suggestion was made to a retiring academic colleague, "How about going back to your village and living the quiet, spiritual life that you had dreamed of?" he replied, insightfully: "*You see, if I go back there, I will be a nobody!*"

The underlying deep-seated fear in one relates to the very essence of one's being. One is afraid of being reduced to a nobody. One craves unconsciously for a sense of importance, an acknowledgment of one's worth by others. When such acknowledgment is not forthcoming, one ventures to create the grounds for it. Could this be the reason why many old people love to narrate, often with endless repetition, their so-called accomplishments to us? They become legends in their own minds.

Why are we in such acute need of a continual reassurance of our own worth? Why can't we just *be*? Why are we ashamed sometimes to simply be ourselves, which means dropping all pretences and image building exercises?

Why are we so afraid of the natural process of aging: the wrinkles in the skin and the greying and falling of hair?

We do not dare confront such questions, because we are afraid of the possible answers.

The courage that it takes to discover that 'I' may well be a 'nobody' is not different from the courage it takes to accept that I have cancer and that I am dying. Once I see it as an absolute fact and accept the implications of this insight, a tremendous transformation is possible in my consciousness. I get awakened, and then there is no fear. There is no more stupidity in resisting reality and in imagining silly legends in my mind.

But, for most of us, the training is otherwise: it is to remain 'magnificently unprepared' for death and impermanence in life.

We smother our secret fears of impermanence by filling our lives with endless noise and activity, and by surrounding ourselves with more and more comforts to which we become addicted. We cling to our various possessions (including human beings) and mundane activities with endless anxiety, for they are our very identity. Without them, would we not be reduced to naught?

We see the pitiable condition of aged people around us. Upset by the unexpected loss of self-importance, uncared for, depressed and defeated, and utterly fearful of impending death, they remain full of yearnings, indulging in self-pity, anger and angst. That may well be our destiny too, unless we *awaken* from our illusions early in life.

Of what avail is it if we can travel to the moon,
If we cannot cross the abyss that separates us from ourselves.
This is the most important of all journeys
And without it, all the rest are useless.

Thomas Merton

4

AWAKENING IN EDUCATION

With regard to education, Galileo observed: "You cannot teach a man anything; you can only help him find it within himself." However, because of the wide gulf between its lofty ideals and what is actually achieved in practice, education has always been an easy target for cynical criticism. Bertrand Russell, for instance, went so far as to say: "Men are born ignorant, not stupid; they are made stupid by education." Will Durant, on the other hand, had this to comment: "Education is a progressive discovery of our ignorance."

These are wise observations indeed, made by some of the most brilliant minds of the Western world. But even these brilliant minds could not apparently envisage a higher dimension to education, the *dimension of awakening*. This, however, was possible in the ancient Oriental world, in India and China, although access to this dimension appeared restricted to but a few. Some of the ancient teachers or 'gurus' and some ancient universities indeed recognized, and gave fundamental importance to, this dimension which formed a philosophical foundation of education. The word 'guru' in Sanskrit literally means *dispeller of darkness*, and refers to an awakened person who is empowered to spread the light of wisdom, based on a direct first-hand realization of spiritual truth.

The 'rational' Western mind will doubtless find it difficult to reconcile the concept of a guru with education. Even if such gurus existed (which is hard to accept in the first place), should not their appropriate place be in religion, and not in education? Amazing as it may sound, such gurus did indeed exist and were in charge of education in India, and that too, some three thousand years ago. Each guru had independent charge of a small 'forest academy' called *gurukul*, where the guru had the complete freedom and authority to teach his students and disciples as he thought best. What the student learnt depended on the student's aptitude and level of competence. Not everyone had full access to the 'highest wisdom' of the Upanishads. Even in the case of those who did have access, only a few could actually arrive at a first-hand realization of that wisdom, resulting in a transformed consciousness.

There is an interesting story about a young student called Svetaketu in one of the Upanishads. His father, Uddalaka, himself a famous guru, sent the boy to another *gurukul* at the age of twelve. When Svetaketu returned home at the age of twenty-four after completing his studies, the alert father was quick to recognize that the young man was full of arrogance of the knowledge he had gained, and clearly not awakened. The son was gradually made aware of the fact that despite all the profound knowledge he had acquired from the Vedas about self-realization, he had still not awakened. Uddalaka then takes over the role of the guru and, during the course of a detailed exposition, gives a brilliant demonstration. The following is a rather dramatized and abbreviated version of the actual story.

Seated below a banyan tree, Uddalaka questions Svetaketu: "How did this huge tree come into existence?" The young man replies readily: "*From the seed.*" "But," asks the guru, "how did the seed come into being?" The young man does not have an answer. So, the guru asks him to go and collect a fruit from the tree, break it open, and take out a seed. Then he asks Svetaketu to break open the seed and to look inside. There is, of course, nothing inside to be seen. But is it just '*nothing*'? Has the huge tree grown out of nothing?

Is it not a miracle that all living forms, including us, have emerged from *formlessness*? What is the nature of that formless essence which contains the universe, and from which space and time and life unfold?

These questions confronted by Svetaketu are as relevant today as they were in ancient times. There are, of course, no ready answers to these eternal questions, and even our most brilliant scientists and philosophers do not have the answers. But it would be foolish to dismiss the questions just because the answers cannot be known. It would be foolish not to be amazed by the sheer miracle of our existence.

Strangely, the more frequently and intensely we feel the miracle, the closer we get to the answers. There are no answers in the conventional sense. The questions themselves dissolve as the observer becomes one with the observed.

The story of how Prince Siddhartha became the Buddha, some twenty-five centuries ago, is one of the most extraordinary and inspiring stories in human history. He was apparently brought up in the lap of luxury, carefully shielded from any exposure to disease, decay, and death. Indeed, a classic case of "a young Apollo 'magnificently unprepared, for the long littleness of life'." Disillusioned by the hollow life of worldly pleasures, Siddhartha set out in search of true meaning in life, but could not come across any genuine guru to guide him.

Here is the story of a true researcher, in a quest for the truth, testing out various hypotheses, receiving many insights, and refusing to fall prey to numerous delusions and temptations that come his way. What persuaded him to carry on without the comforting dependence on any authority, and without any prayer to God? Apparently, it was a simple intuitive faith that truth will prevail, and this faith was strengthened by insights along the way. Mere awakening was not enough for him, and he waited patiently for some ultimate understanding, which did come upon him one fine day. He used the word *nirvana* (extinction of delusion) to describe this state of awareness, the so-called *buddha* nature, which is accessible to one and all. He kept his teaching as simple as possible, addressing the needs of the common people and avoiding philosophical disputation. He said: "*I teach only one thing – there is suffering, and there can be an end to suffering.*"

With the spread of Buddhism, the monk took over the role of the guru and the centre of education shifted from the home of the teacher (*gurukul*) to the monastery. Some of these centres developed into famous universities, the most famous being the one at Nalanda. It was, perhaps, the largest university in the world, with students from different faiths and cultures and a strict merit-based examination system for admission, according to the seventh century Chinese traveler, Huan Tsang. The subjects taught included the Vedas, philosophy, logic, grammar and medicine, in addition to the training in Buddhism given to the novice monks. This renowned teaching centre, managed by wise and saintly monks, eventually fell into ruin, and Buddhism itself practically disappeared from the land of its origin, although it found fresh roots in neighboring countries. The Buddhist and Jain concept of the monastery as a centre of learning was also a feature of Christianity in medieval Europe. This concept was also adopted by various Hindu monastic orders or *mathas* which became centres of learning.

In the best traditional Indian systems, whether based on the *gurukul* model or the Nalanda university model, the fundamental principles, the philosophical foundation based on Upanishadic or Buddhist wisdom were well enunciated. It was recognized that the human problem is essentially one of fundamental ignorance, and that the ultimate purpose of life, and indeed of education, is to discover liberation from this deep-rooted ignorance. The ignorance pertains to the nature of one's self and the inter-connectedness of one's innermost being with that of the entire universe. One is unconsciously trapped into identifying, completely, with a narrow sense of self. This mistaken identity is the root cause of all problems in life, and it denies us the realization that our essential nature is already perfect.

This simple yet profound truth is the basic essence of all Oriental wisdom. Secular knowledge (dealing with worldly affairs and science) and the arts were also valued and developed, but the transient and illusory nature of all worldly phenomena was apparently never lost sight of.

Today, those fundamental foundations of education are conspicuous by their absence.

When the British colonized India, they believed that they were bringing 'civilization' to an ignorant and under-developed nation. Some, like Rudyard Kipling, even believed that there was a "moral obligation" underlying Western imperialism, and a responsibility "to take up the White Man's burden." Insofar as education was concerned, many like Lord Macaulay had no doubts that "Oriental learning was completely inferior to European learning" and, that "a single shelf of a good European library was worth the whole native literature of India and Arabia."

Today, even according to Western standards, India has progressed from the status of an under-developed nation to a developing one – because of, and in spite of Western imperialism. The present system of education in India is almost entirely borrowed from the West, not only in concept, but also in content. It is amazing that, starting virtually from scratch, India has been able to produce educational institutions like the IITs, which are ranked among the best in the world today.

The 'best' of today is, however, significantly different from that in ancient times (Nalanda university, for example). Priorities have changed completely, and there is absolutely no hint in today's education of what was considered to be of the highest priority earlier. The *guru* (dispeller of darkness) has yielded place to the *pundit* (learned scholar). There is now tremendous awareness of technological things related to the material world and, at the same time, appalling ignorance related to man's inner world.

But man does not live by technology alone. "Of what avail is it if we can travel to the moon," as Thomas Merton points out eloquently, "if we cannot cross the abyss that separates us from ourselves?"

We are the hollow men,
We are the stuffed men,
Leaning together,
Headpiece filled with straw.

T. S. Eliot

5

RESISTANCE TO AWAKENING

When Hitler was asked about the secret of the success of his propaganda machine in Germany, he is believed to have said: "The only difference between a truth and a lie is in the number of times you say it." This principle has been effectively put to practice both consciously and unconsciously in society, resulting in all kinds of delusions among us. The delusions lie in mistaking untruth for truth, and illusion for reality. We practice *consciously* when, fully aware of the untruth, we perpetrate the delusion. This is commonly done, for example, in advertising, which is sometimes reduced to a fine 'art' of convincing the innocent customer that he is badly in need of something that he can very well do without. We practice *unconsciously* when we are brainwashed ourselves, and thus transmit our delusions to others unwittingly. We need to awaken from our delusions and, thereby, be free from both types of practices.

The other day, a student visited me after an examination, with a rather long face. He was not well and had apparently done badly. He said to me: "*Sir, I shouldn't have appeared for the exam in the first place, as I had fever. Now, my grades will get affected.*" I tried to comfort him by telling him that whatever is done is done, and that there is no use in crying over spilt milk. But logic does not work when the mind is upset. Then, I tried to tell him that there are more important things in life than grades. He nodded, but kept repeating every now and then: "*But my grades will get affected.*" Then, I spent time trying to show him that he was behaving like a gramophone record gone stuck, and that he was only replaying faithfully something that had been programmed in him. This idea suddenly hit him hard, and the record stopped playing. At the end of our hour-long meeting, he had brightened up considerably, and he left with this thoughtful remark: "*I understand this perfectly now. It is a wonderful revelation. But I'm afraid that I may forget all this when I get back into the rat race.*"

One cannot help but sympathize with the students, for being victims of a drug that has been injected into them since birth. Children are rarely encouraged to discover and pursue interests for which they may have a natural aptitude. They are programmed by their parents into believing that the greatest virtue in life lies in scoring high grades. The parents in turn, have been brainwashed into believing that this is absolutely necessary for achieving success in life.

Children belonging to middle class families in India, for example, are under enormous pressure to become either doctors or engineers, and if the seats for admission to professional colleges cannot be won through merit, they can often be purchased by other means. This obsession with professional education has spawned a big industry, resulting in innumerable coaching centres to help students beat the system of entrance examinations, and a proliferation of private professional colleges for those who fail to beat the system. Education nowadays is big business.

The difficulties in coping with studies and examinations are compounded by the verbal torture that parents often unleash on the poor performers. Comparisons are inevitable within and outside the family, and the poorly performing child is made acutely conscious of his or her inadequacies, and even begins to believe it when the parents say: "You are good for nothing." Naturally, everybody cannot succeed in this mad race. The losers outnumber the winners manifold, and so we end up with a fairly large number of 'good for nothing' individuals in society, thanks to the neurotic delusions of parents.

The so-called 'winners' are not in particularly good shape either. They need to sacrifice much of their childhood and subsequent years in pursuit of something that is important because somebody else said it was. The *joy of learning* is barely experienced in this stressful exercise. The cleverer students are the ones who have mastered the art of beating the system with minimal effort. I know of many bright students who avoid taking the 'tough' (intellectually challenging) courses, and instead opt for the 'easy' ones, only because of the promise of high grades. Many students who are desperate (programmed) to migrate to the United States at any cost, often sacrifice the specializations for which they know they have an aptitude, and are more than willing to settle for anything available. What kind of success is this? The success of delusion?

Today's education is largely reduced to a means of getting a degree, which is considered necessary for survival, or more accurately, for earning a livelihood. This emphasis on livelihood is completely in consonance with the emphasis on *profitability* that drives our modern industries, and is based on the modern world-view that we have inherited from the West. Livelihood, of course, depends on the standard of living, and our modern consumerist culture, as well as the need to promote social standing, ensures that we will always be in need of money to spend on more and more things that we could very well do without.

Thus, as a society, we are driven to finding all possible ways of enhancing our livelihood, and our families at home never raise any questions about the sources of our income, as long as the money keeps rolling in.

Education has obviously done little to stem the growing rot of corruption and erosion of values, which has afflicted all sections of society. Ironically, those who have minimal education seem to be relatively more honest, less self-centred and less deceitful than those with high education. In this connection, Theodore Roosevelt is reported to have said: "A man who has never gone to school may steal from a freight car; but if he has a university education he may steal the whole railroad." One may add that he will probably also get away with it, because a skilled lawyer knows how to make an ass of the law. What education has unwittingly done is to train the mind to be more manipulative and clever, and to give a veneer of sophistication to a personality that is increasingly becoming bereft of character.

Today's education may give us a livelihood, but not necessarily character.

The conspicuous erosion of values in post-independence India and elsewhere in the world has been a cause of concern for many, and educationists are contemplating various ways of somehow injecting ethics into the prevailing system. These are noble attempts, but fraught with difficulties, because they have to be woven into a secular fabric, accommodating the mixed interests of our pluralistic society. Moreover, it is like trying to cure the symptoms, and not the disease. The disease is the cancer of delusion, and even educationists appear to be unaware of the root cause.

If our students are 'magnificently unprepared', it is because our teachers are no less so. And teachers are 'magnificently unprepared' because the only competence sought from them is their academic merit, which is often merely a reflection of their proven ability to get ahead in the academic rat race. 'Awakening' does not figure anywhere as a criterion for selection, and employers appear to be blissfully unaware of it. Indeed, it cannot be fitted anywhere in the curriculum. When academicians are themselves entrapped in the rat race culture, how can they be expected to create the ambience for awakening?

What we need is awakening, and not just 'value education'. What we need is teachers who realize the value of awakening in their own lives, and the rest will follow automatically. The awakened person cannot help but radiate the energy of awakening in all that he or she does. This, of course, does not mean *preaching*. Indeed, in an emancipated society, even children will not take kindly to sermonizing, and justifiably so. However, what can be easily encouraged is simple reflection on why we are the way we are. Awareness of our own programming can be a first step to awakening. Awareness of the initial inner resistance to such reflection is also a part of awakening.

Many people believe that it is the responsibility of religion to account for this aspect of education but, sadly, organized religions have failed to deliver this crucial input that, perhaps, ought to be the focus of all religious practice.

It is unfortunate but true that religion, like education, has also been reduced to a means of serving materialistic ends and encouraging delusion. The higher and common objectives of religion, relating to the surrender of the ego-self to the all-pervading ultimate reality, are lost sight of, and it is only the lower forms of ritualistic worship that are commonly practiced. Being 'God-fearing' is considered virtuous, and it is obviously not recognized that *fear* is an unhealthy basis for any relationship!

God, to many of us, is some kind of a feudal lord to be appeased and worshipped periodically so that He may bless us with all the goodies in life. Such worship, unfortunately, does little to dispel the fundamental delusion and, on the contrary, strengthens the false identification with the ego-self. The differences in our various notions of God, differences in labels, forms, places and types of worship, and our false and sometimes fanatical notions of religious superiority, conversion and re-conversion, sects and sub-sects, unfortunately accentuate the sense of separateness, besides causing endless strife in society.

Once upon a time there lived a guru with a band of keen disciples who could plainly see that their teacher was truly awakened. One day, he asked the students to assemble in a hall on a Sunday evening at 5 p.m. The guru wanted to show the students how to locate Sirius, the brightest star in the sky. After the students had assembled, the guru pointed at a window and said: "Look at that window, and tell me what you see." The students looked and replied dutifully: *"Master, we see the window grill."* "Good!" said the guru, "Now look *through* the window, and tell me what you see." The students looked and answered: *"Master, we see a tree."*

The guru then said, "Now look at the second branch of the tree, and tell me what you see." The students looked and replied: *"Master, we see a bird."* "Excellent!" said the guru, "Now look just to the right of that bird, and tell me what you see." The students looked and said: *"Master, we see two leaves."* "Wonderful!" said the guru, "Now look carefully *through* the gap between those two leaves, and tell me what you see." The students looked and exclaimed in wonder, *"Master, we see a star shining brightly!"* The guru concluded by saying "That, dear students, is the brightest star in the sky. You should now go out, and be able to locate this star in relation to the other stars I had introduced to you earlier."

When the Master died, the disciples took upon themselves the task of spreading his wonderful teaching, ensuring that not one word was missed. Generations passed, and the book containing the teachings became an object of worship, with the words repeated reverently and endlessly. The hall in which he gave his teachings became a pilgrimage centre, and the window grill and all the trees outside became holy symbols to be venerated. Nobody, however, could actually see the star that the Master had talked about, even on Sundays at 5 p.m. But that did not really matter, for the Master and his original disciples had confirmed that it could be seen, and there was no question of the Master being wrong. How wonderful it is to spread the Master's glorious teachings and to baptize the heathen who have not seen the star, and also to vanquish the followers of fake gurus who claim to be able to see the star from other places!

The moral of the above story is very instructive. Today, religion is flooded with rituals whose meanings are little understood, and the religious adherence to these rituals often becomes a serious impediment to awakening. The ritual becomes a prop for the insecure mind – a prop which must be dropped, sooner or later, for the mind to be liberated. Frequently, those who suffer from a compulsion to 'convert' or convince others, do so because this helps in reducing their own insecurity.

But, for many people, rituals are meaningful and the 'path of devotion' is indeed a path that can lead to full awakening, as testified by innumerable saints of diverse faiths. This path is meant to lead to a transformed consciousness, and in the final analysis, it matters little whether one chooses to call it Buddha-consciousness, Christ-consciousness, Krishna-consciousness, or whatever. If, however, one chooses to get stuck on the label, and ends up with hardened divisive notions of *us* versus *them*, as is frequently the case, then there is a clear evidence of delusion. Awakening is simply awakening, and there is nothing uniquely Buddhist, Hindu, Christian, or Muslim about it.

Awakening calls for an alive and open mind, one that does not get stuck on labels. There is nothing wrong with labeling; what is wrong is the complete lack of awareness of the limitations in the labels. No label can completely describe anything, and even if it could, it cannot account for the changes that keep happening to everything. Everything is unique and keeps changing with time; the only thing that gets fixated is our mental idea of that thing. We barely realize this when we look, or rather fail to look, at the common crow or the tree by the wayside. We do not realize this when we unconsciously make sweeping judgments about people, based on their nationality, religion, caste, color, or whatever.

When we awaken, we awaken to our prejudices and we become aware of the endless games played by the mind. But this also requires us to become aware of the tremendous inner resistance to any admission of error.

One of the more serious ailments of the present civilization is its obsession with 'productivity' and the associated illusion of 'progress'. As someone once said: "Passion is good, but not obsession", because obsession results in lop-sidedness and imbalance. You may gain something apparently precious, but at the same time lose something even more precious. Because of this, our obsession with material progress in this technological age has created all kinds of problems. We are hurtling forward at such reckless speed, that unless we slow down and ask *whither* and *wherefore*, it will be difficult, if not impossible, to sustain development of mankind as a whole.

But our obsession with speed remains unchecked. What could be more wonderful than our ability, through the ability of our machines (including computers), to travel at the speed of light? What could be more wonderful than the creation of wealth through unbounded productivity and exploitation of natural resources? Many people strongly believe that 'time is money', whereby addiction to work is worshipped, and doing nothing is abhorred and considered 'a waste of time' (unless it is a meditative exercise meant to recharge one's batteries, so that one can be even more productive). The reality is that *doing nothing* is impossible for most people, and the mind expresses its restlessness through boredom or craving for sensation.

In the academic world, the academician who spends long hours at work, including weekends, is considered a 'role model', especially if his obsession with work results in the publication of a large number of papers. In the corporate world, the manufacturer or salesman who performs excellently in any given period, is expected to outdo this performance the next time and, subsequently, perform even better.

Organizations and individuals are coming to terms with the fact that the demands of modern existence result in various kinds of stress-related problems that adversely affect productivity in the long run. They ask: "What can we do to reduce stress in our hectic lives, and so be able to enhance our productivity?" And in response to this worldwide demand, a wide variety of new-age solutions have mushroomed, with business enterprises successfully marketing them. Many of these techniques are therapeutic in nature, including various types of meditation and breath control exercises, and have proved to be effective. Some of them, however, go a step further and claim a spiritual dimension (quoting ancient wisdom), promising effective methods of tapping into the 'universal intelligence' to achieve any desire, including unlimited wealth. Apparently, the warning of Jesus, "*No man can serve two masters... God and Mammon*" has become outdated in the light of modern wisdom.

Can we have the best of both worlds: cling to delusion and yet find enlightenment? There is a Zen riddle (*koan*) that points at the absurdity of this proposition: *Given that a boat is well-tethered to one shore, how best should one row in order to reach the other shore quickly?*

There is no doubt that as a human species we have made extraordinary progress since the early stages of primitive mankind. But, equally important, it is time that we realized that we have, in this process, lost something precious in terms of *harmony and connectedness with nature.* The following story illustrates this.

An American businessman based in New York, decided to take a break and go on a holiday. He chose to spend a restful week in the Amazon Basin in South America. Every day, he would tour around with the assistance of a local guide. Of course, being a good businessman, his mind would frequently wander from the picturesque and serene surroundings, and work on various possible business schemes. On one such outing, he came upon a native, barely clothed, sitting by the banks of the majestic Amazon river, looking vacantly into the distance. Beside him was a bundle of wood that he had apparently finished cutting, and his bronze body was swathed in sweat. He appeared to be a part of the quiet organic life around him, in harmony with the countless flora and fauna of the rainforest.

After remaining motionless for quite some time, he looked into the water in front of him and soon, with a deft movement of his right hand, dipped into the water and brought up a trout. The fish struggled in his firm grasp, and he waited for it to die. Then, he cut it into pieces with a knife and slowly started eating what was probably his morning breakfast. Every movement, including his eating, was slow and steady, marked by a quiet relaxed concentration.

The American watched all this from a distance, and went across to meet the native. Using his guide as an interpreter, he addressed the native and requested him to demonstrate once again the skilled manner in which he had caught the fish. The native was somewhat perplexed but, nevertheless, obliged. This time he brought out an even larger fish, but as the fish thrashed about in his grasp, he released it back into the waters. The businessman asked: "Why did you release that fish?" and the native replied: *"I've just had my meal. But are you hungry?"* "No, no!" responded the American, "It's just that you have such tremendous talent. If you can catch fish like that, let's say at an average rate of four minutes per fish, and if you worked just six hours a day, you could have a haul of close to a hundred fish in one day. If you get others in your group to help you, it would add up to a fat number." The native was confused, and so he asked, *"What for?"* to which the businessman replied, "Look, I can help you out, and you could make a lot of money." The native was even more confused, and he asked, *"What is money?.."*

We do not know how that story ended, but it is quite probable that the clever businessman had his way, and succeeded in converting the natives. Human history has witnessed many such conversions, and in almost every instance, in addition to obvious material gain, the converters believed that they were doing the natives a great favor, by leading them from backwardness to 'progress', and from darkness to light.

In the modern age, which relies so much on the human ability to think and reason, it is difficult to visualize that these very abilities of thinking and reasoning could be hindrances to a higher level of evolution. Yet, if modern, 'civilized' man is to make real progress, it is necessary to rediscover that dimension of consciousness which 'primitive' human beings and plants and animals have apparently access to, although they are not conscious of it. Awakening implies discovery of this dimension which is latent in the human being, and which provides the link with nature and the universal intelligence.

Nature has been around for ages, and its movements are slow and steady, in contrast to the high-entropic culture of modern man. Unless man is able to pause amid his hectic activities, slow down, and resonate with these movements, it may be impossible to make this discovery. However, the deluded mind, which endlessly seeks fulfilment in the future, will find it difficult to understand that a different kind of fulfilment lies concealed in the present – one that is not ephemeral in nature.

The fact that the vast majority of us live under a delusion can be comforting, but it does not take away either the reality or the enormity of the delusion!

One loves one's spouse, my dear,
but not for the sake of the spouse,
One loves one's sons, my dear,
but not for the sake of the sons,
One loves the gods, my dear,
but not for the sake of the gods,
One "loves" all these, my dear,
but for one's own sake!

adapted from Brhadarnyaka Upanishad

6

ENTRAPMENT BY THE EGO-SELF

The words "one loves one's spouse, my dear..." were supposedly narrated by the sage Yajnavalkya, to his wife Maitreyi, as reported in the Upanishad. Most people may not agree with this apparently extreme perception. It takes some insight to realize the deep truth of this ancient piece of wisdom, which suggests that the nature of one's relationship with others is entirely self-centred. One loves others only when it serves the purpose of one's ego-self. The ego-self may be defined as that entity with which one identifies oneself. It is characterized by a sense of uniqueness that makes one feel an individuality distinct from others.

In those moments of deep conflict when the pleasure the ego-self derives from a relationship turns into pain, love can transform into hatred, although one may be unwilling to accept this harsh reality. Love demands things in return (although one may not be initially aware of it) and is, therefore, *conditional* with the features of an unwritten business contract. For example, parents in their old age demand love and attention from their offspring, and feel 'let down' when this is not forthcoming or up to their expectations. Love can sometimes become an unbearable burden when there is inner resistance to the demonstration of such love as, for instance, in caring for someone chronically ill, merely out of a sense of duty. Similarly, if one's beloved were to be crippled by some terrible ailment or were to die, one would be grief-stricken, but this grief would be centred on the thought: "What will happen to *me* now?"

The bitter truth is that most people, even one's near and dear ones, and even God, serve largely as instruments to satisfy one's ego-self. One thinks well of people who pamper the ego-self; one tends to be indifferent to those who do not make a difference to the welfare of the ego-self; and one is inimical to those who are perceived as inflicting pain to the ego-self. All relationships seem to be conditional. One may experience love or indifference or hatred towards the very same person at different times, depending on the prevailing equation with that person.

One does have occasional glimpses of another kind of love, which has no opposite and which is *unconditional*. But for such love to manifest and sustain, one has to awaken to a dimension beyond the ego-self.

The central message of our ancient teaching, testified by innumerable sages, is this: '*You are not the ego-self that you think you are, and this misidentification is the root cause of all your problems. Awaken from the deep-rooted ignorance related to your identity and find liberation.*'

This, of course, is more easily said than done. In the first place, the vast majority of us are blissfully unaware of this teaching, and it may appear to be rather formidable. Secondly, in this modern age, there is no reason why we should accept such a teaching, which cannot be established by modern science or psychology. Thirdly, even many of those who seem to have a theoretical knowledge of such wisdom are not necessarily awakened.

Above all, the greatest resistance comes from one's own ego-self, and this is something that anyone who practices self-awareness will easily understand. After all, can the ego-self be expected to allow its own annihilation without resistance?

The Buddha's teaching was centred on the problem of human suffering. We may well ask: "*So what?*" Many of us may not consider suffering to be much of a problem, for we tend to associate it with something remote that does not really affect us. We admit to undergoing suffering only in the case of very serious issues, such as the death of someone intimate. There are a few among us, of course, who admit to daily suffering, often due to interpersonal clashes, either at home or at the workplace. The tyrannical boss, or spouse, or mother-in-law is often the culprit, and the ego-self assumes a victim-identity.

But we will do well to understand suffering in a much broader context. Whenever we feel a sense of discomfort or even indifference, we suffer. Thus, one suffers whenever one is worried, afraid, angry, upset, irritated, frustrated, jealous, hurt, impatient, anxious, agitated, stressed, suspicious, or just plain bored. Who then can claim to be free of suffering? Not only do we all suffer, we do so fairly frequently. We suffer not only when we are wide awake, but also in our dreams when we sleep. However, one can truly claim to be totally free of suffering during the few moments when one is drawn into the 'deep sleep' state of consciousness. Upon waking up, one can recall that during those blissful moments, characterized by freedom from any kind of suffering, there was also freedom from the notion of the ego-self.

On reading this, the ego-self may immediately protest: *"So what? If there is no ego-self, then life is not worth living."* We would much rather put up with suffering than give up our sense of ego-self, our identity, our very *raison d'être*! Besides, who would do any work if there was nothing for the ego-self to gain?

What is the stuff that one's ego-self is made up of? One's physical appearance, personality, possessions, achievements, affiliations – these are the things that commonly define one's ego-self. In every society, there is a sense of power associated with these attributes, the value of that power depending on the value-system practiced by that society.

To understand the nature of the value-system, it is instructive to observe what it is that one's genuine well-wishers look forward to see in oneself. Commonly, it is the enhancement in the power of the ego-self. In professional life, this means climbing the ladder of success quickly. For example, in academic institutions, it is not uncommon to have non-teaching staff wishing young faculty members: "One day you may become the Head of the department, and perhaps even a Dean, and if you are really lucky, maybe even the Director." This well-intentioned remark reveals the prevailing value system. The Director has more value than a Professor, who in turn has more value than a Technician. Such a value system, unfortunately, prevents employees from looking at one another as simple human beings (having only different roles to play), and creates false notions of superiority and inferiority. These notions tend to harden, and the false notions of superiority can result in delusions of grandeur, which when deflated by circumstance, can result in much suffering.

There are instances of relatively young Professors rising quickly to the top position of Director, and on completing their terms, choosing to resign, to avoid the ignominy of returning to their former positions as ordinary Professors and interacting with their former friends (and now, inferiors). In the rat race, the positions of the rats in the front line appear to be the most desirable, but these positions are often the most precarious. Intense suffering is unavoidable if one tries to cling to such positions, resisting the inevitable.

Finally, some of us may look down on the rat race and the materialistic world, and believe that we are 'spiritual' and relatively free of the ego-self. Such a belief itself gives one a sense of selfhood, which is the harbinger of delusion.

One feels an enhanced sense of selfhood whenever an event occurs to increase one's power in relation to others, and this can result in much happiness and a sense of self-fulfilment. We may refer to such happiness as *ego-pleasure*. A diminished sense of selfhood, on the other hand, can cause much suffering.

One man's ego-pleasure is invariably another's suffering or 'ego-pain'. Ego-pleasure is inherently fragile, somewhat like the flame of a candle, vulnerable to the winds of circumstance. The thrill of possessing a new car or winning a coveted award can be easily deflated by the news of the neighbor buying a more luxurious car or winning a more prized award! The larger the thrill of ego-pleasure, the greater is the agony of ego-pain. Often, the very objects that contribute to one's ego-pleasure later become sources of ego-pain. Pride can turn into shame and love into hatred. We cling to the sources (objects) of ego-pleasure, and resist the sources of ego-pain.

The sequences of various pleasures and pains are like peaks and troughs in the waves of the ocean. The waves are numerous and endless, having varying amplitudes and frequencies. The ocean is, in fact, an archetypal image reflecting the basic problem of human existence (*samsara sagara* in Sanskrit), with many meanings. One such meaning relates to the delusion in identifying the self with the ocean wave, which is tossed and turned relentlessly by the tide of time. Wisdom lies in discovering the vastness, immensity, and stillness in the depths of the ocean, and this enables one to deal effectively with the ego-ripples on the surface with detachment and responsibility. The ripples will always be there, but one is no longer entrapped by the belief that the ripples constitute the totality of one's existence.

Entrapment by the ego-self happens because of various

kinds of programming that take place in us. The obsession with productivity in today's world, for example, implies getting productive work done by everybody, and various management techniques are resorted to, both consciously and unconsciously. The 'carrot-and-stick' is one such approach, widely prevalent. One needs to offer a 'carrot' (an incentive for the ego-self that gives it an enhanced sense of selfhood) or else give the 'stick' (a punishment that will hurt the ego-self and diminish the sense of selfhood) to get work done. Such an approach, although very effective, unfortunately serves to reinforce the delusion of identification with the ego-self.

We thus program ourselves to be ruled completely by desire and fear and, thereby, prevent ourselves from accessing an infinitely larger domain of consciousness. Indeed, if an enlightened soul were to tell us, from his or her own first-hand experience, that it is possible to find fulfilment in a life free from desire and fear, we would find it impossible to accept. It is like the story of the proverbial 'frog in the well'.

Surely, all of us have discovered, at some point or the other in our lives, the sense of fulfilment we get from engaging in creative activity, for no incentive or disincentive (carrot or stick), but for the sheer pleasure in doing it? The 'joy of learning' is a fine example of this. In such activity, which is quietly performed to perfection, one does not need certification by others to realize the value of one's work. The joy is felt instantaneously in the present, not something that waits for acknowledgment or a prize in the future. How wonderful it would be if one could fill one's daily life engaging in such activity, at least for some time, if not most of the time! Is this possible?

Most of us have been programmed into believing that it is not possible. Some may even be inclined to argue that, in order to excel, there must be competition for a prize, and that the greater the value of the prize, the better the performance is likely to be.

The Taoist sage, Chuang Tzu, had this to say about such delusions:

When an archer shoots for nothing, he has all his skill.
If he shoots for a brass buckle, he is already nervous.
If he shoots for a prize of gold, he goes blind,
Or sees two targets – he is out of his mind!
His skill has not changed, but the prize divides him.
He thinks more of winning than of shooting,
And the need to win drains him of power.

The importance of keeping the morale high is well recognized in today's world, and individuals who can inculcate this in others are recognized as good managers. Smiling at people, listening patiently to their grievances, giving them a pat on the back every now and then – these are now increasingly recognized as being very important and effective, and a reflection of 'emotional intelligence'. However, beyond a point, they only serve to enhance delusion, and this is something that the science of modern management has failed to recognize. If awakening from delusion is considered important, then we must realize that all these techniques are only ways of stroking the ego-self. The widely popular principle, *I'm OK, you're OK*, is fine if one accepts delusion to be OK. Otherwise, if we consider awakening to be important, then what we need an increasing awareness of is the fact: *I'm deluded, you're deluded.*

Indeed, awareness of delusion is the first step to awakening. Unfortunately, we do everything possible not to wake up! The more we delay awakening, the more we get entrapped by our ego-selves and, consequently, the more painful awakening will appear to be. And so, even when we are faced with the ultimate reality of death, we do our best to cling to delusion. Using the same old management techniques, we tell the dying person: "No, no, please don't get depressed. Don't think of death. You're OK. Everything will work out just fine."

Thus, we engage in sleepwalking, with no intention of awakening, all the way until death.

One may be surrounded by great beauty,
By mountains and fields and rivers.
But unless one is alive to it all,
One might just as well be dead.

Jiddu Krishnamurti

7

THE POWER OF AWARENESS

The power of thinking is well recognized, but not so the power of awareness. We may talk of two dimensions of awareness: that of one's 'inner' world and that of the so-called 'outer' world, although at the deepest level, the distinctions of inner and outer tend to dissolve. Indeed, the quality of awareness depends upon its depth and intensity. Most of us are unaware, or at best, superficially aware of what is going on inside us and around us, and this is because we are entrapped by our ego-selves all the time. Some degree of freedom from the ego-self is necessary to enable both inner and outer awareness.

Awareness of the great beauty around us, expressed so powerfully by Krishnamurti, is a fine example of the outer kind of awareness, which very few people seem to be able to access. Inner awareness is a powerful means of gaining access to the workings of the ego-self and, thereby, penetrating the thick veil of delusion created by it. Freed from the obsessive notion of the ego-self, a *quiet joy* is felt – an inexplicable joy which is similar to the one experienced at the time of awareness of 'great beauty'.

Let us first examine outer awareness, or rather the lack of it, in our lives.

When one's baby cries, one tries different ways of comforting it. One may try to divert the child's attention by pointing at something – a bird, for example, and one may exclaim: "Look at that bird!" and the infant looks. It sees something interesting, something alive and new. Captivated by what it sees, it forgets all about crying. In those moments of full awareness, the child is one with the bird. It is in communion with something joyful, something that defies description. One could call it the *essence* of all life.

It is amazing, but this trick works with the little child, not once or twice, but several times. It works even when the child is not crying. Every time the child's awareness of the bird is awakened, it can see newness, and be part of a wonderful aliveness. But as the child grows older and 'matures', it loses that ability. The grown-up child is no longer fascinated. A dead label takes the place of a live bird.

As we grow older, we gather more and more of such labels and lose touch with living reality. We recognize things, but we don't really see them. We don't waste time listening to the song of a bird, or observing the quivering of leaves in a tree. We never pause to see the ever-changing colors and moods in the sky. Nor do we ever hear the endless rhythmic orchestra of crickets. We have more important (productive) things to do. But even if there is nothing to do, we are not able to notice or relish the wondrous life all around us. We have unconsciously trained ourselves not to look, especially at surroundings that are familiar, no matter how beautiful or serene they may be. A never-ending stream of thoughts holds us captive, and our mental world of make-believe is far removed from the immediate physical reality around us. We fail to see and feel the ever-present beauty and serenity. We miss the essence.

We fail to feel the aliveness around us, not because there is no aliveness, but because something in us has apparently died. It died, or perhaps went to sleep early in our lives, and nobody warned us about it. Nobody told us that it was a precious thing that we needed to hold on to, to nurture and to deepen awareness of.

To be 'child-like' is not only to be wonderfully alive, but also to be carefree, playful and innocent. We can see these attributes in nature, in plants and animals. These creatures live entirely in the present. Every action – even the seemingly erratic flight of a butterfly – is a movement in spontaneity, a celebration of life. Little wonder then, that sages and poets recognize a sense of *sacredness* in the child-like state. "Heaven lies about us in our infancy", wrote Wordsworth in one of his many poems on childhood. It is a heaven that we can plainly see in *all* little children, and it is amazing how it makes absolutely no difference whether the infant is born in the lap of luxury or in abject poverty. Jesus talked of the need to be like a little child in order to "*receive the kingdom of God*". The *essence* that we glimpse in our early childhood is imbued with a spiritual grace. It is an untutored spirituality that comes to us naturally, a spirituality devoid of labels.

The quiet joy that comes from simple aliveness, from being conscious of a vibrant universe, is a gift from nature to all living creatures. It is a *present* that can be realized only in the present. But somehow, we keep denying ourselves this gift. Somehow, we have been made to believe that the present is not good enough for us, and that we need to improve our condition so that we can find happiness in the future. No doubt, we need to do plenty of things for improvement, but we need not deny ourselves the gift of simple aliveness in the present.

Let us now turn to inner awareness.

Inner awareness manifests in looking calmly at oneself, like a witness, with detachment, without judgment, and without intervention. It is almost like scientific observation, except that there is no labeling and theorizing. Awareness is a dynamic activity, always in the present. It is perhaps more like looking at oneself through the eyes of God – not a frightening and judging God, but an omnipresent and compassionate one.

Our normal mode of consciousness is usually characterized by a complete lack of awareness. We are not in touch with what is really going on inside us moment-to-moment, because our attention is unconsciously projected outward. There appears to be a need for conscious motivation on the part of the 'subject' to choose itself as the 'object' of attention. Indeed, the very fact that this is possible suggests that one's essential reality (subject) is distinct from one's ego-self (object). This object manifests as thought and emotion, and when the ego-self disappears, even momentarily from the field of attention, one remains in a state of 'pure consciousness', which is the ultimate reality that is referred to repeatedly in our ancient teaching. The discovery of this ability to treat one's own ego-self as an object of attention is the beginning of inner awareness.

However, the ego-self usually ensures that this awakening does not happen by keeping the mind preoccupied with relentless mental activity all the time. It is as though we are possessed by something over which we have little or no control. Eckhart Tolle points out in his insightful book *The Power of Now* that we are not very different from some so-called "mad" people we occasionally encounter in the streets, always jabbering to themselves. We know that most of this jabbering is nonsensical and repetitive, and we pity such people, not realizing that we too do the very same thing, although in a more sophisticated manner. Our jabbering is covert, within the confines of our brains, not perceptible to others! There seems to be no way by which we can switch off this apparently meaningless mental activity, and we engage in it even when we sleep (i.e. in our dreams). It is only when we are totally exhausted that all *mental noise* ceases, and we enjoy a few blissful moments of deep sleep.

Why are we apparently addicted to such compulsive mental activity? It seems as though the ego-self fears the danger of extinction and the only way to ensure its continued survival is through relentless and often 'mindless' activity. There is a deep sense of insecurity in its very existence, and it has to make its presence felt somehow, all the time. Awareness can reveal this insecurity, whenever the notion of the ego-self is threatened. This is revealed by the reactions of the ego-self in the form of boredom, anger, jealousy, hurt, worry, etc. These reactions are accompanied by characteristic manifestations in the physical body and one learns to recognize these signals. The mind may say, "*I am not angry*", but the body's reaction will expose the lie.

Awareness is the art of seeing instantly what is really going on, without actually interfering or controlling it. The very seeing can bring about a transformation, if the awareness is intense. It is as though a shift in identity takes place. One no longer identifies fully with the ever-changing and passing clouds of one's thoughts and emotions, and instead finds oneself linked to a much larger dimension: the background space of pure consciousness in which these clouds come and go.

Then, the habitual resistance to the apparent cause of insecurity, and its manifestation in the form of anger, jealousy, hurt, or fear subsides and often vanishes. One may even be able to smile at oneself, watching the antics of the manipulative ego-self. Suddenly, it does not matter so much if someone called one an idiot, for indeed only an idiot would react so idiotically! In the acceptance of the present, the ego-self surrenders and there is peace. As long as the ego-self resists the present reality – and this could be anything, the heat of the summer or a rival getting a promotion – there is insecurity and suffering. The moment one becomes aware of this, and the awareness spots the resistance (which is the ego-self in operation), there is either a total or partial release, which brings relief along with a strange sense of freedom and harmony. This is in consonance with a basic principle in mechanics: *When a restraint is released, the reaction ceases to develop.*

On the other hand, in the normal state of consciousness, one may continue to resist, and consequently, the inner reaction builds up. What began as a minor irritation can explode into a violent rage. Or else, it is repressed within oneself and one feels terrible throughout the day, and often transmits one's depression to others. This pattern of behavior often repeats itself, and one can find oneself re-enacting the same or similar dramas, as is commonly done in many homes. If any one partner in a warring relationship discovers the power of awareness, the whole pattern of the relationship can take a magical turn for the better.

Awareness reveals, for example, moments of hatred against the very person with whom one had thought one was in love. Anybody that appeals to the ego-self or pampers it is a 'good' person. As for the person who does not pander to the desires of the ego-self or who dares question or obstruct it, 'there's something wrong with him'. One stores these hurts in one's subconscious mind, and sooner or later takes 'sweet revenge'. There may be a periodic outpouring of all the accumulated agony stored in the mind, with a graphic description of every historical detail, and this may take the other person by surprise (for there may have been no intention to hurt in the first place).

Awareness reveals that the real seeds of anger are rooted within oneself; external circumstances merely provide opportunities for the expression of the angry ego-self.

If one is unaware, it is often impossible even to recognize that one is in fact suffering. The violent reaction of the ego-self produces the delusion that one is doing a great job by setting things right and teaching others a lesson. In this regard, the Buddha had this to say: "*When your house is on fire, would you choose to run after the person who may have caused the fire, or would you try to save your house from destruction?*"

The great insight that follows an awakened awareness is that the root of all mental suffering is within oneself. However, most people do not recognize this, and are fooled by their ego-selves into believing that the cause is invariably external in nature. The awakened person is also subject to this conditioned response of the ego-self, and may also feel the anger and hurt, but these feelings of distress do not eclipse the underlying awareness that the real problem is within oneself. The wise person is one who does not trust the response of the disturbed mind, and who chooses to wait for the disturbance to subside. The greater the awareness, the more rapidly will the feelings of distress subside.

The ego-self, fearful of the precarious nature of its existence, strives to fill the void created by insecurity with more and more possessions and identities that promise enhanced stature, security and permanence (*my* bank balance, *my* lovely house, *my* handsome physique, *my* beautiful wife, *my* award-winning patent, *my* wonderful trip to Europe, *my* son at IIT...). But it is like filling a black hole; nothing is ever enough, and the insecurity pops up again and again. One tries to fight boredom with anything that can give more sparkle to one's life. One goes on a holiday, or experiments with one's love life, but the initial thrill does not last long, and the boredom and emptiness return along with a craving for sensation.

Life suddenly becomes interesting when someone elopes with somebody else's wife; and one loves to gossip about such things. One loves to have drama and intrigue – TV serials and movies are designed to provide food to satisfy and promote this craving.

Awareness exposes the image that the ego-self attempts to project constantly in front of others. Whenever people meet, they do not really meet! The meeting is between different projected images, and a great drama is enacted, with the actors not realizing that they are acting (unless they are *awakened*). Awareness can bring a great sense of freedom from this relentless image-building exercise, and one can be oneself without any fear or need for drama (*'What will he or she think of me!'*). Awareness exposes the many manipulations of the ego-self, to be in the good books of important persons, and to show rivals in poor light.

Interactions with so-called rivals can be very revealing: they are invariably 'win-lose' situations, when one operates in the unconscious mode. When one 'wins', one basks in a false expansion of the ego-self, and when one 'loses', it is a loss of some 'self-esteem'. Arguments are born from the need of the ego-self to assert that it is right, and admitting to a mistake reflects a significant loss of ego-self. However, the practice of awareness takes away this unconscious compulsion to be always right.

The continual practice of awareness is bound to bring freedom from the entrapment of the phantom ego-self. But this is not easy, and the first objection that most people who have not experienced awakening will raise is: *Will there then be any life left worth living?*

Does this question arise in your mind? Do you recognize what it is in you that poses this question, and why it does so?

The birds have vanished into the sky,
And now the last clouds fade away.
We sit together, the mountain and I,
Until the mountain remains.

Li Po

THE LIGHTNESS OF BEING

Li Po's poetic words express succinctly and wonderfully how awareness, when it is deep and intense, leads to a dissolving of the ego-self. The poet does not attempt to describe the feeling that ensues in this state of consciousness, which is not easily expressible in words. It is a quiet joy, a 'peace that passeth understanding.'

Whenever the burden of psychological baggage of the ego-self is released, one experiences a lightness that is delightful. In contrast, the presence of the ego-self introduces a heaviness that one carries around unconsciously. Sometimes, this is reflected in the posture and bearing, especially in people who are habitually full of a sense of pompous greatness. The heaviness becomes particularly pronounced when one is subject to some mental or emotional burden, some suffering caused by the ego-self. When this burden lifts, and one cheers up, one feels the lightness.

Lightness is, therefore, associated with cheerfulness and joy. *Light* is associated with wisdom that dispels the darkness of ignorance. These two different meanings are combined in the word *enlightenment*, which is the outcome of awakening, and which implies a *lightening* of the burden of the ego-self through the *light* of awareness.

The statement of Descartes, "I think; therefore I am", made some four centuries ago at the dawn of the 'age of reason', has been hailed by many in the West to signify some very profound realization. But is there not some delusion in the suggestion that it is one's ability to think that reveals the nature of one's being? What happens when thinking comes to an end? Does one cease to exist?

Spiritual masters indicate the contrary, and suggest that it is only then that one is able to realize one's innermost nature, free of all notions and beliefs. This does not prevent one from thinking and, indeed, one can think with far greater clarity and alertness without the usual distractions. The awakened person would, therefore, prefer to modify Descartes' statement as simply: "I am." One may also add: "I can also think, when required."

The state of *I am* may be referred to as the state of simply *being*. It is contrasted by the state of *becoming* which is the state commonly experienced by human beings, driven by their ego-selves. 'Living in the present' is associated with the state of being. The ego-self has no room for existence in such a state, and that is why it drives us into the future, in pursuit of happiness that seems missing in the present. One is always seeking to *become* something other than what one *is*, and this seeking never seems to stop. The present moment then serves merely as a means to reach the future, where there is the promise of a sustained survival of the ego-self. Sometimes, the ego-self chooses to escape from the present, not into the future but into the past, where it strengthens itself through an identity 'stored' in memory.

Apparently, the state of becoming is our normal mode of consciousness. However, this should not prevent us from accessing, at least occasionally, the precious state of being. This is what awakening does, and it enhances our quality of living. For the fully awakened person, the state of being, in fact, takes over as the normal mode of consciousness, and pivoted on this state, all action is directed. In the state of being, marked by the absence of the ego-self, there is a feeling of oneness with the universe, a slowing down and, sometimes, cessation of mental activity. Centred in this state, it is possible to use the ability to think most effectively and creatively, whenever required. In the state of becoming, on the other hand, the ego-self is in full command, and there is relentless mental activity. Sometimes, it appears as though instead of thought being a tool for one to work with, one becomes a tool for uncontrolled thinking: *The master becomes the slave.*

Who is the thinker behind one's endless stream of thoughts? What is the source of the energy that goes into thinking? Indeed, what is the source of the energy that sustains life in the living body? What makes the heart beat so regularly, and maintains the various systems in the body? What is the source of energy that maintains other organisms, and even so-called 'inanimate' matter, which is also loaded with energy? What is it that creates, maintains, destroys and transforms energy in its various forms in the Universe? This is a mystery that we apparently can never understand, but one that we can and, indeed, must experience continuously. We are then flooded with a magnificent sense of awe and wonder.

The following is a description of a simple experience of awareness that anyone can access in daily life.

One awakens in the early morning to the songs of the birds in the trees. One remains lying down, just listening to the greetings of nature. There are thoughts of a hundred chores that try to interfere with this listening, but one recognizes that this is the ego-self trying hard to assert its phantom existence. One smiles and continues listening, enjoying the full-throated calls of different birds, the scurrying of squirrels, and the chorus of the crickets in the deep background.

One gets up, splashes water on one's face and enjoys the tingling sensation. One then goes out for a walk, often accompanied by one's spouse or child or a friend. One greets the other with a genuine sense of joy, and maybe touches the other's hand or caresses the face. During the walk, words are sparingly used. One breathes in the fresh air of the early morning, takes in the sounds and smells of nature, as one observes the changing hues in the surroundings with the coming of dawn. Mental noise makes its appearance now and then, and one allows this to happen without controlling it.

As one walks, one feels the pleasantness of the earth beneath one's feet, and the softness of the breeze caressing the skin. There is a spring in one's gait, and one feels the lightness of being. One observes flocks of birds, flying or gliding effortlessly in the sky. The sky itself looks wonderful, lit up with changing hues that look like liquid brush-strokes of a magnificent painting, one that is alive. The blueness of the sky, viewed through the dark branches and green leaves, emphasizes the beauty of the trees. One has seen this spectacle several hundred times before, but every time it is new, fresh, and original. The leaves on the trees, some of them glistening with the morning dew, flutter and wave in the breeze, and one acknowledges the greeting that nature seems to be sending out, and waves back.

In those moments of unalloyed joy, characterized by the complete absence of the ego-self, one truly experiences a kind of sacred state of being, of aliveness and oneness with everything else.

This kind of an experience takes one close to one's innermost being, in which the sense of ego-self is dissolved, although temporarily. Indeed, it is readily accessible to every one of us, freely available and totally inexpensive, although there is no advertising agency to market it. It is truly one's home, to which one can return periodically, even in the din and bustle of daily life. One just has to look out of the window, or observe one's breathing, or caress any object (even a paperweight) to return to that state of being.

One becomes aware of the rhythm of life, in the changing seasons, the waxing and waning of the moon, the rising and setting of the sun, and also in one's own thoughts and even in one's breathing. One discovers that when the mind is free of the agitated ego-self, breathing and thinking both slow down. Applying this principle in its converse, one can consciously choose to breathe slowly and deeply, in order to calm oneself and return to the state of being. This practice turns out to be particularly beneficial when one finds oneself to be agitated.

Our gurus have always advocated deep breathing as an exercise in meditation. Every time one breathes out slowly after taking in a deep breath, one may even consciously visualize that one is getting released from the habitual tendency of clinging and grasping. In that pause between inhalation and exhalation, as in the interval between two thoughts, one comes to rest in a state of surrender and peace. Indeed, one day, not very far from now, the body will die and there will be no new inhalation or thought to take in, and that would be fine.

No doubt, on hearing this, the ego-self will protest: *"At least you should be worried about the welfare of your kith and kin, if not all those unfinished projects for which you are responsible!"*

In the first place, 'worrying', which is a favourite activity of the ego-self by which it ensures its continuity in time, does not do anyone any good. It cannot solve any problem; in fact, it is *the* problem. Secondly, all responsibility ceases when the basic energy required to discharge responsibility itself ceases. Last, but not the least, is the big delusion of the notion of 'doership', the belief that the ego-self is the 'doer'.

There are some wonderful analogies in traditional wisdom that describe the delusion underlying the widespread notion of doership. The 'lizard analogy' shows us how silly it would be for a lizard on the ceiling to imagine that it is supporting the weight of the roof. The 'rice grain' analogy similarly shows us how deluded it would be for the grains of rice, jumping about in a boiling pot of water, to believe that they are the creators of their wonderful kinetic energy! But this is exactly the way the ego-self behaves. It does not realize that even the little energy required for its own precarious existence comes from another source – an infinite, intelligent and mysterious source. The ego-self, in fact, usurps all the energy available (comparable to the contents of a small pot of water floating in the vast ocean), and claims ownership to it. In this connection, it is interesting to note that the word *ahankaram* in Sanskrit, which is commonly understood to mean *arrogance*, literally means 'doership by me'. Not many of us are aware of this etymological link between the notion of doership and arrogance.

Unfortunately, the forces that govern the present civilization strongly encourage the delusion of doership in almost every sphere of activity. The notion of 'intellectual property' that has shot into prominence in recent times is but a manifestation of this disease. However, through awareness one can gain liberation from this fundamental delusion, realizing the subtle inter-connectedness and mysterious workings of the vast energy field that runs everything. The big dreams in life are still achievable, and indeed can be achieved far more efficiently, but they are no longer motivated by delusion, and are no more important than the 'little things' in one's daily life.

As Jesus put it: "*Consider the lilies of the field, how they grow; they toil not, neither do they spin.*" One may also add:

'Consider also how they die, when the time comes, with no clinging and no remorse.'

What would you do if you came to know, somehow, that you have just one more hour to live? Would you just panic and become mortally afraid?

What would you do if, instead, you discovered that you had some more time – a day or a month or even a year left to live? Would you just go on a splurge, spend all your savings, and enjoy all the good things in life while you still can? Or would you bemoan your fate and worry yourself to death? Most 'responsible' people are expected to worry endlessly about the future of their dependants, and if you worry yourself to death in this process, it may even be considered respectable. Maybe you would buy up a whole lot of life insurance, if that were possible? Or would you suddenly turn religious, and devote your remaining time to a piety that you had never really felt before, out of the present fear of the unknown future?

Or, if you could devote your time to understanding what it really means to *die* – would you finally address that one question that you have fearfully evaded all your life?

The fact is that one could die any moment – and this could be an hour, a day, a month, a year, or several years from now – and one is totally unprepared to face such an eventuality. But should one choose to *awaken*, perhaps death may no longer be as fearful as it appears. When it comes, one may be able to receive it with a quiet dignity, like an autumn leaf falling from a tree. One will also then be able to live life with the same quiet dignity.

To see the world in a grain of sand
And heaven in a wild flower,
Hold infinity in the palm of your hand,
And eternity in an hour.

William Blake

9

THE LITTLE THINGS IN LIFE

The world may be in a total mess and yet, paradoxically, everything is perfectly in its proper place. This may sound absurd and, yet, this is exactly how one feels in the awakened state. One is aware of this apparent dichotomy not only in the so-called external world, but also within oneself. On the surface there may be chaos, but strangely, in the depths of one's being, one feels a wonderful peace and a sense of order. And one can also see this perfection in nature, all around oneself.

One sees it in the quiet dignity of the common wildflower and the common crow. One feels a wonderful bond with all these creatures and with everything else. One can see the universe in the tiniest dewdrop. One can sense that the blood that flows through one's veins is not different from the sap that rises through the plants. It is the same energy, the same miraculous life-force, the same formless essence underlying all forms. That essence never dies, even though the outer forms keep changing and atoms keep rearranging themselves, according to the natural law.

Wise sages of our ancient past, as well as modern physicists, tell us that everything is basically interconnected and nothing can happen without the participation of everything in space and time. The occurrence of any event is the outcome of complex individual and collective *karmic forces*; it cannot be otherwise. Things are the way they are because we are the way we are. We can and, indeed, should try to set things right at the outer level, but this may not always be possible. Yet, strangely, there is nothing to set right at our deepest level; there is already wonderful peace and harmony. More importantly, one senses the working of a primordial intelligence, which cannot be understood by the human intellect.

There is nothing wrong with our big dreams in life, but it is wise to see them in proper perspective. There is nothing wrong with planning for the future, but it is wise to recognize that it is worrying that often *masquerades* as planning. There is nothing wrong with thinking, but it is wise to be aware of the compulsive mental activity that operates in the guise of thinking. There is nothing wrong with judging, but it is wise to discover detachment to one's mental positions.

There is nothing wrong with anger or jealousy, but it is wise to recognize that these are expressions of one's suffering. There is nothing wrong with ritualistic worship, but it is wise to see the deeper meaning in the ritual. There is nothing wrong with disbelieving in God, but it is wise to see that disbelief is also another kind of belief. There is nothing wrong in keeping secrets or telling lies, but it is wise to realize that there is, perhaps, an omnipresent intelligence at work and the notion of privacy is but a myth.

There is nothing wrong with wanting to be important, but it is wise to see the delusion. There is nothing wrong in seeking fulfilment in the outer world, but it is wise to see that true fulfilment can be found only in one's innermost being. In the words of Jesus: "*The kingdom of heaven is within you.*" The following verse by Kabir is a poignant expression of this wisdom:

Musk lies hidden inside the musk-deer,
But the deer searches for it all over the forest.
Likewise, God resides in our innermost being,
But we search for self-fulfilment in the external world.

But, of course, this wisdom will have little appeal to a person with very strong desires, and one may have to travel a long way before making this discovery for oneself. For others, who are blessed with limited desires, and are able to bring the light of awareness into their consciousness, the discovery can be immediate. The pull of delusion will nevertheless be present, and one must learn for oneself the art of balancing, of 'living *in* the world, but not *of* the world'. Every situation poses two alternative paths: *the path of delusion* and *the path of awakening*. One will find oneself straying into the path of delusion, because that is the unconscious way of the world, but continual awareness and first-hand experience of the lightness of being shows the way to freedom.

There may be many things lacking in the present, but the only sensible thing to do is to accept the reality, and get on with whatever task that needs to be done. If there is some knowledge or skill that has to be acquired, an awakened person just gets on with the job using the power of thinking efficiently, as one uses a tool, and this can be quite joyful. In the intervals between various tasks, one discovers the art of resting in the lightness of being, and this enhances one's working efficiency and injects creativity in one's work. Indeed, one is continually aware of that source of all energy, which is allowed to operate through oneself with minimal interference from the ego-self.

Awakened, one is liberated from the 'carrot-and-stick' approach of the world, and so does not need the usual incentives to do one's job. One just does what is required with a quiet contentment, and without anxiety regarding the outcome. This approach indeed enhances the quality of the outcome. One may be showered with worldly success, but, for the awakened person, it is like 'a cloak that rests lightly on one's shoulders'. Things may go wrong occasionally and one accepts the reality, quietly and gracefully, and tries to learn from the experience. One is not afraid to speak one's mind, but develops a healthy detachment to one's own mental positions. One is not worried about making mistakes and will not evade responsibility. One recognizes that suffering arises from resistance to the reality of the present.

Above all, one recognizes the important role of suffering in one's awakening. It is like pain in the body: a signal that something is basically wrong with one's health. The pain is identified as being rooted *within* oneself and, hence, the 'setting right' needs to be done by oneself, on oneself. Nobody else can resolve one's problems. Even the slightest irritation has a silent message to convey, and an awakened person is one who recognizes the import of this message. One is aware of the root cause of one's problems, and is alert to the manipulations of the ego-self, which is always trying to assert itself, sometimes by means of a clever 'backdoor' entry.

The awakened person is alert to the habitual tendency of the ego-self to interpret facts by building imaginary stories around them. The stories reflect the 'judgments' of the ego-self, and reveal its fears and desires. There may be some measure of truth in these judgments, but the awakened person is able to view these with detachment and compassion.

How often we get hurt because somebody 'did not have the decency' to respond to an invitation, or return a call, or acknowledge a favor. The awakened person does not get hurt by such behavior patterns, because they are recognized as programmed responses of one's ego-self, and also because one is able to empathize with the other person's position. Even when the so-called crime committed is of a more serious nature, there is a quiet acceptance of the fact and one will make an appropriate response, but it will not be motivated by feelings of revenge. Sometimes, the most appropriate course of action is to do nothing, reposing faith in Nature to take its own intelligent course. The awakened person knows only too well that the root cause of all crime is *ignorance*, and thus will put to practice the dictum of Jesus: "*Forgive them, for they know not what they do.*"

The awakened person can be of tremendous help, when suffering people seek counsel. The type of counsel depends on the perceived maturity and state of mind of the suffering individual. What the suffering mind generally seeks is *solace*, some balm for the wounds inflicted on the consciousness. But words and deeds of solace provide only a temporary relief, and suffering born out of deep-rooted delusions of the ego-self will recur. The awakened counsellor will attempt to point to this reality, wherever possible. Of course, this may not always be possible, and when 'ignorance is bliss', it may be 'foolish to be wise'.

Having tasted the joy of awakening, one cannot help but transmit this awakening, wherever possible, to others. Just as one who is bound to the ego-self will invariably attempt to impose bondage on others, the awakened person who is free from the ego-self will enable freedom in others. Freedom cannot be given externally, of course; it has to be discovered through an inner awakening. One will then discover the power of *acceptance* (of the present reality) and the power of *surrender* (of the ego-self's desires). One will then discover the 'guru' within one's innermost self.

One discovers the art of discriminating between two different states of happiness: the joy that springs from the lightness of being (enjoying little things, like watching little children at play or being encaptured by a beautiful sunset) and the ego-pleasure that arises from some accomplishment (some success, like winning a prize). One learns to value the former, and to be wary of the latter which is but an exercise in self-aggrandizement. One also discovers that the joy that arises from the state of being does not have an opposite, unlike the ego-pain associated with failure.

Having tasted the power and grace of the 'meditative' dimension, one trains oneself to return to it again and again, and to be aware whenever that dimension is lost by the movement of the ego-self and drowned in the cacophony of mental noise. One can actually observe this happening, for example, while getting drawn into petty gossip, and one can see how one's power and energy easily get scattered. One learns the art of being aware of this and of remaining detached and inwardly still, centred in the state of being.

One discovers that the little things in life are no less important than the big things. One tries to give complete attention to every task at hand, whether it be something as trivial as brushing one's teeth or as important as performing a surgical operation. The Zen Masters are renowned for this attitude of 'mindfulness', as revealed by this piece of wisdom given in a text on Zen Buddhism:

The Master simply pursues excellence
in whatever he does.
He makes little distinction between
his work and his play,
His labour and his leisure,
his mind and his body,
His education and his recreation,
his love and his religion.
He hardly knows which is which,
for he is always doing both.

One does not have to 'work' all the time, and there are wonderful opportunities to practice awareness, to interact with nature and, thereby, strengthen one's realization of the state of being and the underlying oneness with the universal energy. When one is commuting to work or when one is waiting in a queue, one relaxes and quietly observes with alertness whatever enters one's field of consciousness.

One looks quietly at human beings and observes their activities, conscious of the tendency of the ego-self to pass judgment. One looks, for example, at the salesman in the shop or the waiter who serves a meal, and pauses to observe the person as a human being, rather than just a means to fulfil one's end. Through such quiet observation, one accesses the underlying kinship and the other person may also be enabled to feel this. On the occasions when one may be provoked to angry reaction, one is aware instantly of one's suffering and one discovers creative ways of handling it, recognizing the root of the problem. One also recognizes the suffering in others and finds creative ways of compassionate healing.

One looks closely at the ants, the birds, the squirrels, the clouds, the trees, and also little children, and one marvels at their natural state of being filled with innocence and dignity. One imbibes and radiates their joy and affection. In those quiet moments that come to one, often unexpectedly, one discovers a spaciousness and depth in one's awareness. Forms appear and disappear in that space, and sounds come and go in that silence, but there is a powerful inner stillness that remains.

One discovers the extraordinary in the ordinary.

Not in imagined futures,
Or in remembered pasts,
But only here and only now
Will you find a peace that lasts.

Kirtana (*Meet me*)

ABOUT THE AUTHOR

Dr. Devdas Menon had his schooling at St. Xavier's, Kolkata, and his engineering education in civil/structural engineering at IIT Madras and IIT Delhi. After a few years of industry experience and a teaching career at NIT Calicut, he has been with the Department of Civil Engineering at IIT Madras, Chennai, since 1998.

At the age of twenty-five, he underwent a profound inner transformation that was to leave an enduring impression on him. He withdrew from the material world for a brief period and, under the guidance of some Himalayan masters, came to realise that there was no need at all to 'renounce' the world. On their advice, he chose to remain in and practice the profession for which he had been trained.

Dr. Devdas Menon is known for his research work and publications on concrete structures and rapid affordable housing, as well as his popular textbooks on Reinforced Concrete Design, Structural Analysis and Advanced Structural Analysis. He has contributed to the development of national standards, and is presently the Chairman of the Bureau of Indian Standards CED 38

Committee on Special Structures. He is also well-known in the industry as a structural design consultant.

In addition to his contributions in teaching, research and development in civil engineering, Dr. Devdas Menon has a special interest in holistic education. He has conducted several workshops for students, teachers and corporate organisations on finding meaning and fulfilment in life through self-awareness and inner transformation. His lectures on this topic (available on YouTube) have been very popular, and have transformed the ways in which students look at their education and career paths. Prof. Menon has also designed and teaches two unique 'free elective' courses on Self-awareness and Integral Karmayoga, which have gained popularity among students from various disciplines at IIT Madras.

In recognition of his wide-ranging contributions, he was conferred the Distinguished Service Award by the IIT Alumni Association in 2013, the Best Teacher award by IIT Madras in 2014, and the Outstanding Concrete Engineer award by the Indian Concrete Institute (Chennai Chapter) in 2014.

For more information, visit: www.devdasmenon.com

For further details, contact:
Yogi Impressions LLP
1711, Centre 1, World Trade Centre,
Cuffe Parade, Mumbai 400 005, India.

Fill in the Mailing List form on our website and receive, via email, information on books, authors, events and more.
Visit: www.yogiimpressions.com

Telephone: (022) 40115981, 22155036
E-mail: yogi@yogiimpressions.com

Join us on Facebook:
www.facebook.com/yogiimpressions

Join us on Instagram:
www.instagram.com/yogi_impressions

ALSO PUBLISHED BY YOGI IMPRESSIONS